You Are a Masterpiece

You Are a Masterpiece: God's Promises for Mental, Physical, and Spiritual Strength

Copyright © 2024 Joel Osteen

All rights reserved. No part of this book may be reproduced or transmitted in any form or by any means, electronic or mechanical, including photocopying, recording, or by any information storage and retrieval system, without permission in writing from the publisher.

Scripture quotations marked AMP are taken from the Amplified® Bible (AMP), Copyright © 2015 by The Lockman Foundation. Used by permission. lockman.org.

Scripture quotations marked ESV are taken from The ESV® Bible (The Holy Bible, English Standard Version®). © 2001 by Crossway, a publishing ministry of Good News Publishers. Used by permission. All rights reserved.

Scripture quotations marked GNT are taken from the Good News Translation in Today's English Version - Second Edition Copyright © 1992 by American Bible Society. Used by Permission.

Scripture quotations marked MSG are taken from *The Message*, Copyright © 1993, 2002, 2018 by Eugene H. Peterson. Used by permission of NavPress. Represented by Tyndale House Publishers.

Scripture quotations marked NIV are taken from the Holy Bible, New International Version®, NIV®. Copyright © 1973, 1978, 1984, 2011 by Biblica, Inc.™ Used by permission of Zondervan. All rights reserved worldwide. www.zondervan.com The "NIV" and "New International Version" are trademarks registered in the United States Patent and Trademark Office by Biblica, Inc.™

Scripture quotations marked NKJV are taken from the New King James Version®. Copyright © 1982 by Thomas Nelson. Used by permission. All rights reserved.

Scripture quotations marked NLT are taken from the *Holy Bible*, New Living Translation, Copyright © 1996, 2004, 2015 by Tyndale House Foundation. Used by permission of Tyndale House Publishers, Carol Stream, Illinois 60188. All rights reserved.

ISBN: 978-1-951701-61-1

Printed in the United States of America.

Created and assembled for Joel Osteen Ministries by
Breakfast for Seven
breakfastforseven.com

For additional resources by Joel Osteen, visit JoelOsteen.com

Table of Contents

YOUR MENTAL STRENGTH / 9

YOUR PHYSICAL STRENGTH / 49

YOUR SPIRITUAL STRENGTH / 85

From the very title of this book, "You Are a Masterpiece," I want you to know one undeniable truth — you are an incredible creation. God made you unique, with a divine purpose and a bright future! The Scripture says: *For we are God's masterpiece. He has created us anew in Christ Jesus, so we can do the good things he planned for us long ago.* (Ephesians 2:10, NLT)

It might be hard to believe, especially when you feel less than or the world's expectations weigh on you. But trust me, you truly are God's masterpiece, and this book is here to remind you of that truth.

Imagine each page as a little push, a nudge to help you take that next step forward. I want you to get this down in your spirit: you are made for greatness. You have what it takes to push through!

And there's more. This book is about more than reading. It's about doing, feeling, and believing in yourself. It's about taking what you discover here and using it in your everyday life.

Throughout these pages, you'll be encouraged with God's promises for your mental, physical, and spiritual strength. Let them be a gentle reminder that, no matter where you are or what you're going through, you are created by Almighty God. He has you in the palm of His hand!

So let's walk this journey together, believing in the masterpiece that is you. Keep praying, keep moving forward, and know this in your spirit: you are a masterpiece!

MENTAL

1 Your Mental Strength

You will keep in perfect peace those whose minds are steadfast, because they trust in you.

ISAIAH 26:3 / NIV

Almighty God calls you a masterpiece! He has equipped, empowered, and anointed you. So, does it really matter what your mind focuses on? Absolutely.

I like to look at it this way: Your mind is the driver of your life. Your thoughts are the steering wheel. And your life is going to go in a positive or negative direction, depending on how you think.

Joshua 1:8 tells us that those who meditate on God's word will prosper and have good success.

But too often, negative thoughts come against us. They fill us with doubt, fear, and negativity. That's why in this section about your Mental Strength, I'll share tips and insights you can use right away, including:

- **Thoughts Are Powerful:** Discover the incredible power you have to shape your future simply by being mindful of your thoughts.
- **Protect Your Mind:** Learn ways to keep out bad thoughts and let in positive, faith-filled ones.
- **Thoughts Lead to Actions:** Understand that what you think can guide what you do.
- **God's Word Helps You to Think Right:** Let God's Word get down on the inside, and you're going to see God's goodness in new ways.

As we spend time in the promises of God, let's commit to filling our minds with thoughts that uplift, inspire, and move us forward.

Remember, by being mindful of your thoughts, you can direct your actions, steering your life toward your God-given destiny.

1 / FROM NEGATIVE TO POSITIVE THOUGHTS

You are a masterpiece with a powerful, disciplined mind. It's how God created you. But no matter how good of a person you are, no matter how much faith you have, you'll never get to the place where negative thoughts don't come.

Discouraging Thoughts

- My dream is never going to come to pass.
- I'll never meet the right person. It would have happened by now.

Worried Thoughts

- The medical report wasn't good.
- My child is off course.
- Business is slowing down. What am I going to do?

The enemy's main tools are deception and lies, and your mind is the bullseye of his target. If he can control your thinking, he can control your life. You can't stop negative thoughts from coming. But . . .

2 / JUST BECAUSE A THOUGHT COMES TO MIND DOESN'T MEAN YOU HAVE TO THINK IT.

You control the doorway to your mind. You're in charge of what you give access to. That's why the Scripture tells us to guard our mind:

> *Be careful how you think; your life is shaped by your thoughts.*
> Proverbs 4:23, GNT

Be selective of what you allow in. If the thought is negative, discouraging, bringing worry and fear, do yourself a favor, and don't let it in. It's not complicated. Don't dwell on it. Don't give it the time of day. Nobody can make you think something. The enemy can't force you to dwell on his lies. He has to deceive us into opening the door. Too often, when these negative thoughts come, we don't think twice. We just allow them access. We go around worried, discouraged, intimidated. Start paying attention to what you're dwelling on. Don't let thoughts in such as: "Nothing good is in my future. Why do I even have my hopes up? I'm going to be disappointed again."

3 / IF IT'S NOT POSITIVE, HOPEFUL, ENCOURAGING, AND EMPOWERING, THEN IT'S NOT FROM GOD.

That is the enemy doing what he does best . . . trying to plant negative seeds, fearful seeds, inferior seeds in your thinking.

*You, L*ORD*, give perfect peace to those who keep their purpose firm and put their trust in you.* Isaiah 26:3, GNT

What is your mind stayed on? What are you dwelling on throughout the day? You may be thinking, "Joel, have you watched the news? Interest rates going up, inflation, the stock market . . . I'm worried." Those are all valid thoughts. **I'm not saying to deny reality. I'm saying to be selective in what you dwell on.** The right approach is, "Yes, there's a lot of uncertainty. I don't know how it's all going to turn out. But God, I know You're my provider. Just as You take care of the birds of the air, You'll take care of me." Instead of keeping your mind stayed on your problems, stayed on the news, stayed on doubt, stayed on worry. Keep it stayed on what God promised you. Here's a simple principle:

4 / WHEN A NEGATIVE THOUGHT COMES, ERASE IT AND REPLACE IT.

It's not enough to just not think negative thoughts. Once you dismiss it, once you make the decision, "I'm not dwelling on that. I'm not allowing that worry in," the problem is, in a few seconds, those negative thoughts will come back: "Here I am again, just reminding you that it's never going to work out." Once you erase the negative, replace it with a positive thought. Don't leave your mind empty. The negative thought comes, "Nothing good is in my future. It's all downhill from here." Dismiss it. Don't give it the time of day. Then take the next step, "Father, You promised the path of the righteous, my path, gets brighter and brighter."

The way of the righteous is like the first gleam of dawn, which shines ever brighter until the full light of day.
Proverbs 4:18, NLT

You said my latter days will be better than my former days.

"Your beginnings will seem humble, so prosperous will your future be." Job 8:7, NIV

When the negative thoughts come, "The problem is too big. The opposition is too strong. The addiction is too great, you'll never get past it . . . " you could let those thoughts play and live defeated, discouraged, intimidated . . . Or you can replace them with what God says:

- "Father, You said when the enemy comes against me one way, You would defeat them and cause them to flee seven ways."
- *"The LORD will cause your enemies who rise against you to be defeated before you. They shall come out against you one way and flee before you seven ways."* (Deuteronomy 28:7, ESV)
- "Lord, this may be too big for me, but I know it's not too big for You."
- *"Ah, LORD GOD! Behold, You have made the heavens and the earth by Your great power and outstretched arm. There is nothing too hard for You."* (Jeremiah 32:17, NKJV)

DO THIS
Find a scriptural promise for an area you've struggled in and commit it to memory.

5 / NEVER THINK NEVER

What about when the "never" lies come? Lies that tell you, "I'll never get well, never meet the right person, never get out of debt." Don't let that play in your mind. If you do, you're defeating yourself. That's keeping you from seeing God's favor. Erase it, that's the first step. "I'm not dwelling on that anymore." Then take the next step and replace it: "Father, thank You that what You started in my life You will finish. What I'm up against is not permanent. I know this too shall pass. Breakthroughs are coming, freedom is coming, healing is coming, victory is coming!" **Get your mind going in the right direction, and your life will go in the right direction.** You're going to draw in what you're constantly thinking about. If you're thinking "can't do it" thoughts: "I'm not enough. This problem is too big," you're drawing in defeat. That's making you weaker. Your gifts are being pushed down. Your faith is being diminished. Why don't you try erasing and replacing? How much further will you go, how much happier will you live if you'll guard your mind? How much more of God's favor will you see if you'll be selective in what you're dwelling on?

The Scripture says:

> "This Book of the Law shall not depart from your mouth, but you shall meditate in it day and night, that you may observe to do according to all that is written in it. For then you will make your way prosperous, and then you will have good success."
> Joshua 1:8, NKJV

MENTAL

"Get your mind going in the right direction, and your life will go in the right direction. You're going to draw in what you're constantly thinking about."

–Joel

Meditate means "to think about over and over." Worry is meditating. It's letting the negative play again and again. Some people have that principle down. They are professional meditators. The problem is, they're meditating on the wrong thing. They're letting the negative continually play. Maybe that sounds familiar. Why don't you switch what you're meditating on? It doesn't take any more energy to believe God's Word than it does to worry. This one small tweak can make a life-changing difference. Instead of going through the day worried about your future, wondering how you're going to make it, make a small tweak. Meditate on what God says: Father, thank You that You have me in the palm of Your hand.

> *"Behold, I have engraved you on the palms of my hands; your walls are continually before me."* Isaiah 49:16, ESV

I know You're ordering my steps.

> *The LORD makes firm the steps of the one who delights in him.* Psalm 37:23, NIV

You said no good thing will you withhold because I walk uprightly.

> *For the LORD God is our sun and our shield. He gives us grace and glory. The LORD will withhold no good thing from those who do what is right.* Psalm 84:11, NLT

You said You would work out Your plan for my life.

You will do everything you have promised; LORD, your love is eternal. Complete the work that you have begun.
Psalm 138:8, GNT

Now, instead of your thoughts defeating you, draining your energy, limiting your future, you're using your thoughts to encourage you, to empower you, to build your faith. Maybe today you say, "Joel, I'm worried about my child. He's off course, running with the wrong crowd. That's why I can't sleep at night. That's why I'm upset." I know that's hard. I know how much you love your child, but worrying is not making it better. Living stressed is not helping him or you. The reason you don't have peace is because your mind is stayed on the problem. Your mind is stayed on what's not working out. God said, if you'll make a switch, if you'll keep your mind stayed on Him, if you'll think positive, hopeful, faith-filled thoughts, then He will give you peace in the midst of the problem. Instead of dwelling on all the negative, on what might happen, why don't you use that same energy to meditate on what God promised you? Father, You said, my children are mighty in the land. You said the seed of the righteous is blessed.

His descendants will be mighty on earth; the generation of the upright will be blessed. Psalm 112:2, NKJV

You said that as for me and my house, we will serve the Lord.

"But if you refuse to serve the LORD, then choose today whom you will serve. Would you prefer the gods your ancestors served

beyond the Euphrates? Or will it be the gods of the Amorites in whose land you now live? But as for me and my family, we will serve the LORD." Joshua 24:15, NLT

Negative thoughts are going to come, but if you'll learn this principle to erase and replace, then you won't give in to the worry, the fear, the discouragement.

DO THIS
Start your day in gratitude by writing a list of things you are thankful for.

6 / DWELL ON GOD'S GOODNESS

When you wake up in the morning and your thoughts whisper, "It's going to be a lousy day. I have so many problems. I don't feel like going to work." You could dwell on that, believing that it's true. But you'll go around discouraged, defeated. It will become a reality. You'll have a lousy day. A better approach is to say, "No, thanks. I'm not going to dwell on those discouraging thoughts. They came to my mind, but I know I control the doorway. I don't have to allow them in. I'm going to erase them and replace them with some better thoughts. This is going to be a good day. It's another day that the Lord has made. Father thank You that I'm alive. Thank You that You woke me up this morning. Thank You that I'm healthy. Thank You that You have a bright future in store for me." The apostle Paul said:

> *Fix your thoughts on what is true, and honorable, and right, and pure, and lovely, and admirable. Think about things that are excellent and worthy of praise.* Philippians 4:8, NLT

- You can't think negative thoughts and have a positive life.
- You can't think sickness and have health.
- You can't think lack and have abundance.

The battle is taking place in your mind. Be selective of what you allow in. Imagine someone shows up at your house and knocks on your front door. You open it, and there is this stranger. He is carrying an axe, a hammer, a rifle, a bag of poison . . . all of these harmful, dangerous things. You wouldn't say, "Hey, come on in! Make yourself at home! Good to see you! There's some food in the fridge." No, you wouldn't think twice. You would tell him, "You're not welcome here. You need to get off my property." You would shut the door, dead bolt it, and make sure he left. Your mind is your house. It's where you live. There's nothing more valuable, more important, more sacred. That's your property. You have complete control over what you let in. You can't stop it from coming. It may knock on the door, but you don't have to give it access. Next time fear knocks with thoughts of, "You'll never get well. You saw the report. This sickness is the end." Why don't you say, "No, you're not welcome here. I will live and not die. God is restoring health unto me."

7 / WHEN FEAR KNOCKS, LET FAITH ANSWER.

Next time doubt shows up and you worry, "It's too big. It's never going to work out. I don't have the connections. I'm too old." Just say, "Sorry, you have the wrong address. There's no place for you here."

"Before I shaped you in the womb, I knew all about you. Before you saw the light of day, I had holy plans for you…"

JEREMIAH 1:5 / MSG

When insecurity comes knocking, "I'm not good enough. I'm not attractive. I don't have a good personality. Nobody wants to be around me . . ." I say this respectfully, don't you dare let those thoughts in! Your attitude should be, **"Get off my property. You're not welcome here. I know who I am. I'm a masterpiece."**

> *For we are God's masterpiece. He has created us anew in Christ Jesus, so we can do the good things he planned for us long ago.* Ephesians 2:10, NLT

I'm one of a kind. I'm made in the image of God.

> *So God created mankind in his own image, in the image of God he created them; male and female he created them.* Genesis 1:27, NIV

I'm crowned with favor.

> *Surely, LORD, you bless the righteous; you surround them with your favor as with a shield.* Psalm 5:12, NIV

I'm wearing a robe of righteousness.

> *I will greatly rejoice in the LORD; my soul shall exult in my God, for he has clothed me with the garments of salvation; he has covered me with the robe of righteousness, as a bridegroom decks himself like a priest with a beautiful headdress, and as a bride adorns herself with her jewels.* Isaiah 61:10, ESV

I am fearfully and wonderfully made.

> *For you formed my inward parts; you knitted me together in my mother's womb. I praise you, for I am fearfully and wonderfully made. Wonderful are your works; my soul knows it very well.*
> Psalm 139:13–14, ESV

Start closing the door of your mind to the negative. Close the door to these destructive, limiting, defeating thoughts. Sometimes we've believed them so long, they've become a part of who we are. We didn't know any better. It's how we were raised. We opened the door, and now it's like those negative thoughts have taken up residence. They have their own room. Imagine fear, worry, doubt, and insecurity all living in your house. They are dragging you down, stealing your joy, taking your peace. That may be the way it's been, but this can be a new day. You need to evict some tenants that have been living in your mind. The good news is, you're in charge. They may seem bigger, stronger, more powerful, but you determine what stays in your mind. You need to tell fear, "You're evicted. You're not welcome here anymore." I'm not living afraid of what might happen. My future is in God's hands. Nothing can stand against Him."

You need to tell worry, "You've been with me long enough. I'm sorry, you've lost your lease." You need to tell doubt, "Your time is up. I've got some new rules. You have to go." You need to tell insecurity, "Sorry, there's no more place for you. You're out of here. See you, not going to be you." All the negative that's weighing you down and limiting your future, why don't you serve some eviction notices? Keep your mind positive, hopeful, full of faith, expecting good things, believing to overcome, trusting God to do what only He can do. What I've learned is, when your mind is filled with the positive, there's no room for the negative. When you're full of faith, praise, gratitude, believing for the best, then when the negative comes (and it will), you don't even answer the door. You don't pay it any attention.

8 / FEAR KNOCKS, BUT THERE'S A "NO VACANCY" SIGN. THIS MIND IS FULL OF FAITH.

Complaining and discouragement knock: "Sorry, no vacancy. This mind is full of praise." "Father, thank You for what You've done. Thank You for fighting my battles. Thank You for surrounding me with favor. Thank You for making ways where I didn't see a way." When worry comes, "What about these gas prices? Did you see the news? Inflation? Recession?" "Sorry, no vacancy. Father, thank You that You're Jehovah Jireh, the Lord my provider. The economy is not my source. My job is not my source. You are my source. I know I'm connected to a supply line that will never run dry." This is not just being positive. This is releasing your faith. This is what allows God to do awesome things. When your mind is stayed on Him, you're going to have peace in the middle of a pandemic, favor in a famine, strength in the storm, going up when you should be going down.

DO THIS
Plan in advance the truth you will declare when fear and worry come knocking.

This is what my mother had to do. She was diagnosed with terminal liver cancer in 1981 and given a few weeks to live. She was only 46 years old. She had been perfectly healthy. Always active, working in the yard, pastoring the church, traveling the world with my father. Suddenly, she got this terrible news. She became so frail. She weighed eighty-nine pounds. Her skin was very yellow. The doctors said there was nothing they could do. You can imagine the negative thoughts that came knocking at her door: *This is it. You're done. Make plans for your funeral.* In the middle of the night when she couldn't sleep, the thought came, *You can wear that new pink dress you bought to be buried in.* My mother had good reasons to feel worried, afraid, hopeless, but she understood this principle.

- When fear knocked, she didn't let it in.
- When worry knocked and said, "It's over, quit believing." She said, "You're not welcome here."
- When doubt knocked, "You heard the report. They're the best doctors in the world, and there's nothing they can do." She said, "No thanks, there's no room for you in my thinking."

She guarded her mind. She was extremely selective of what she allowed in. She knew she was in a fight. She wasn't about to give her valuable real estate — her mind — any room for negative, discouraging, defeating thoughts. When you are in a battle, when forces are coming against you in a great way, that's when you will be most tempted to believe the lies and get discouraged. "It's never going to work out, just accept it." At that time, more than ever, you need to close the door. Don't give those lies access. You need all your energy to believe, to stay strong, to have faith to overcome what's trying to stop you. Be diligent.

> *And do not give the devil an opportunity [to lead you into sin by holding a grudge, or nurturing anger, or harboring resentment, or cultivating bitterness].* Ephesians 4:27, AMP

That means, don't give him any rooms in your house. Don't give him any place in your thinking. My mother didn't just erase those negative thoughts, she replaced them with God's Word. She kept her mind filled with God's promises. All through the day, she went around quoting scripture, saying: "I will live and not die."

> *I shall not die, but I shall live, and recount the deeds of the LORD.* Psalm 118:17, ESV

"God is restoring health unto me."

> *"For I will restore health to you, and your wounds I will heal, declares the LORD because they have called you an outcast: 'It is Zion, for whom no one cares!'"* Jeremiah 30:17, ESV

"With long life He will satisfy me."

> *"I will reward them with long life; I will save them."* Psalm 91:16, GNT

If you leave your mind empty, it's going to naturally gravitate toward the negative, especially when you're in difficult times. That's when you need to be very disciplined about what you allow in. And on purpose, think thoughts of hope, faith, healing, victory.

A friend of mine had cancer. He was a professional football player. He had to stop playing to take the treatment. He had worked so hard to get to this point, now this huge disappointment. He could have been discouraged, given up on his dreams, but his attitude was, "This thing is not going to defeat me. It's just a bump in the road. I will play football again. I will accomplish my God-given dreams." He was so disciplined to guard his mind. He wouldn't let anyone use the word "cancer" in his house. He told his family, his friends, even his doctors, he didn't want them speaking that word over him. He didn't want it down in his spirit. When he was taking chemo, he stayed positive, "Father, thank You that I am healed.

> *But he was pierced for our transgressions, he was crushed for our iniquities; the punishment that brought us peace was on him, and by his wounds we are healed.* Isaiah 53:5, NIV

" . . . greater is He that's in me than what's coming against me."

> *You are of God, little children, and have overcome them, because He who is in you is greater than he who is in the world.* 1 John 4:4, NKJV

Two years later, against all odds, he was back in the league, playing professional football. Thoughts told him all the reasons it would never

MENTAL

"If you're facing something today, don't let those lies take root. Don't give them access by believing them. Dwell on what God says about you."

—Joel

happen, but he didn't answer the door. He gave no place to the enemy. If you're facing something today, don't let those lies take root. Don't give them access by believing them. Dwell on what God says about you.

My mother kept doing this. It didn't happen overnight, but little by little, she got better and better. Medical science even tells us that when people are positive and hopeful, when they believe they'll get well, they're much more likely to recover than those who are negative and discouraged. My mother will be 90 years old this year, healthy and whole. She went from a few weeks to live to forty-four years. God has the final say. Why don't you get in agreement with Him?

Don't let those lies play in your mind. Start erasing them, and then take the next step, replace them with faith-filled, favor-filled, victorious thoughts. Here's a key: You're moving toward what you're constantly thinking about. This can be helpful, or it can be harmful. "Joel, I never get any good breaks. The pandemic set me back. I wish I had more talent." If you're constantly thinking negative thoughts, you're moving toward defeat, lack, and mediocrity. Try a new approach. "Favor is in my future. Good breaks are chasing me down. The right people are headed my way. Father, thank You that the best part of my life is in front of me." When you think like that, you're moving toward favor, increase, open doors, and abundance. What do you think about your health? Are you thinking about the negative? "I've had this addiction for years. Everyone in my family struggles with depression. I'll never get back in shape." That's moving you in the wrong direction.

9 / CHANGE STARTS IN YOUR THINKING.

How about trying this approach? "This addiction is not permanent. Chains that have held me back are being broken. I am free. I am whole. I am healthy. I am in shape. I am attractive. I am full of energy, vitality, and strength. My youth is being renewed like the eagles." Get your mind going in the right direction. Your life is going to follow your thoughts. Set your mind and keep it set (Colossians 3:2). At the start of the day, you need to set your mind. When you get out of bed, "Father thank You for the gift of this day. It's another day that You have made. I'm going to choose to be happy, I'm going to see the best. I'm going to be a blessing to someone. I'm going to live this day to the full."

If you don't set your mind, the enemy will set it for you.

You'll wake up and think about all your problems and everything you've done wrong: "I'll never break this addiction. I should have eaten better yesterday. I can't believe that coworker was rude to me." Don't start the day off negative. Don't bring yesterday's trouble, yesterday's disappointment, yesterday's failures into today. Start the day afresh and anew. The Psalmist said, God's mercies are new every morning.

> *"Through the LORD's mercies we are not consumed, because His compassions fail not. They are new every morning; great is Your faithfulness."* Lamentations 3:22–23, NKJV

DO THIS
Create a simple morning routine that starts your day in peace and prayer.

"I know who I am. I'm a masterpiece. I'm one of a kind. I'm made in the image of God. I'm crowned with favor. I'm wearing a robe of righteousness. I'm fearfully and wonderfully made."
—Joel

It's not every afternoon or every evening. Every morning, receive the new mercy. How you start the day, many times, will determine what kind of day it's going to be. Don't ever start the day in neutral. Don't wait to see what kind of day it's going to be. Determine what kind of day it's going to be.

Make up your mind:

- This is going to be a good day.
- I'm going to be productive.
- I'm going to enjoy my family.
- I'm going to honor God.
- I'm grateful to be alive.

That's setting your mind. That's making plans for a blessed day. Set your mind and keep it set. That implies things will happen that will try to unset it.

Challenges, delays, people that are rude, doors that close . . . You can't stop it from happening, but you can choose to not let it get on the inside. When worry comes, "No, my mind is set. God is still on the throne. He's in control of my life." When offense comes, you could get upset, live bitter. No, "God is my vindicator. He's fighting my battles." The contract doesn't go through. You don't get the position. You could be down, disappointed, but your mind is set. "God, I trust You. I know You wouldn't have closed that door unless You had something better in store." Don't let the challenges during the day unset your mind. Keep it set. Keep it stayed on Him. Keep it full of praise, keep expecting good things, keep believing for what God promised.

I talked to a man who was moving to Houston from another city. He got a promotion that he'd been believing for. It was a dream come true. He had to sell his house before he could buy a house here. The problem was the real estate market in his city was very depressed, hardly anything was selling. On his street alone, there were four houses for sale, and many more in the neighborhood. Thoughts came, telling him all the reasons his house wouldn't sell, and the job wouldn't work out: "The market is soft. There's too much inventory. This isn't the right time." He was tempted to get discouraged, to think it could not happen, but he understood this principle. When doubt knocked, he said, "No thanks, you're not welcome." When thoughts of worry came, "What if it doesn't work out? What if you miss this great opportunity? What if you can't move?" He said, "Sorry, worry, you don't belong here. I don't have space for you." He kept his mind filled with faith: "Father, I know You can make a way, where I don't see a way. Thank You that You're causing my property to stand out, that Your favor surrounds me like a shield."

> *Surely, LORD, you bless the righteous; you surround them with your favor as with a shield.* Psalm 5:12, NIV

The real estate agent told him that, on average, it was taking over a year for properties to sell, not to get his hopes up. All of the facts said it would be months and months, but two weeks after he put the house on the market, it sold for full price. He met with the new owners and asked why they chose his house out of all the others. They said, "We looked at over thirty houses, but when we walked in yours, something just felt right. We knew it was supposed to be ours."

God knows how to bring the right people to you. He knows how to open doors you can't open. He knows how to turn your child around, how to free you from that addiction. Don't believe those lies that say, "It's not going to happen. It's too late. The odds are against you." Just say, "No thanks, you're not welcome here. I'm going to keep my mind stayed on Him." There's a battle taking place in your thinking. Start closing the door to the negative. You control the access. Be selective. Don't just let anything in. Wrong thinking will keep you from your destiny. Start erasing and replacing.

Erase the negative. Don't give it the time of day. Replace it with God's Word, with positive, faith-filled thoughts.

If you'll do this, I believe and declare, because your mind is stayed on Him, you're going to have more peace, more joy, more favor. Forces that have held you back are being broken. You're about to rise higher, accomplish dreams and go further than you've ever imagined, in Jesus' name.

YOUR MENTAL STRENGTH, GOD'S MASTERPIECE

The way of the righteous is like the first gleam of dawn, which shines ever brighter until the full light of day.
PROVERBS 4:18, NLT

"Your beginnings will seem humble, so prosperous will your future be."
JOB 8:7, NIV

"The LORD will cause your enemies who rise against you to be defeated before you. They shall come out against you one way and flee before you seven ways."
DEUTERONOMY 28:7, ESV

"Ah, LORD GOD! Behold, You have made the heavens and the earth by Your great power and outstretched arm. There is nothing too hard for You."
JEREMIAH 32:17, NKJV

"This Book of the Law shall not depart from your mouth, but you shall meditate in it day and night, that you may observe to do according to all that is written in it. For then you will make your way prosperous, and then you will have good success."
JOSHUA 1:8, NKJV

"Behold, I have engraved you on the palms of my hands; your walls are continually before me."
ISAIAH 49:16, ESV

The LORD makes firm the steps of the one who delights in him.
PSALM 37:23, NIV

For the LORD God is our sun and our shield. He gives us grace and glory. The LORD will withhold no good thing from those who do what is right.
PSALM 84:11, NLT

You will do everything you have promised; LORD, your love is eternal. Complete the work that you have begun.
PSALM 138:8, GNT

His descendants will be mighty on earth; the generation of the upright will be blessed.
PSALM 112:2, NKJV

"But if you refuse to serve the LORD, then choose today whom you will serve. Would you prefer the gods your ancestors served beyond the Euphrates? Or will it be the gods of the Amorites in whose land you now live? But as for me and my family, we will serve the LORD."
JOSHUA 24:15, NLT

Whatever is true, whatever is noble, whatever is right, whatever is pure, whatever is lovely, whatever is admirable — if anything is excellent or praiseworthy — think about such things.
PHILIPPIANS 4:8, NIV

For we are God's masterpiece. He has created us anew in Christ Jesus, so we can do the good things he planned for us long ago.
EPHESIANS 2:10, NLT

So God created mankind in his own image, in the image of God he created them; male and female he created them.
GENESIS 1:27, NIV

Surely, LORD, you bless the righteous; you surround them with your favor as with a shield.
PSALM 5:12, NIV

I will greatly rejoice in the LORD; my soul shall exult in my God, for he has clothed me with the garments of salvation; he has covered me with the robe of righteousness, as a bridegroom decks himself like a priest with a beautiful headdress, and as a bride adorns herself with her jewels.
ISAIAH 61:10, ESV

For you formed my inward parts; you knitted me together in my mother's womb. I praise you, for I am fearfully and wonderfully made. Wonderful are your works; my soul knows it very well.
PSALM 139:13–14, ESV

And do not give the devil an opportunity [to lead you into sin by holding a grudge, or nurturing anger, or harboring resentment, or cultivating bitterness].
EPHESIANS 4:27, AMP

I shall not die, but I shall live, and recount the deeds of the LORD.
PSALM 118:17, ESV

"For I will restore health to you, and your wounds I will heal, declares the LORD . . ."
JEREMIAH 30:17, ESV

"I will reward them with long life; I will save them."
PSALM 91:16, GNT

But he was pierced for our transgressions, he was crushed for our iniquities; the punishment that brought us peace was on him, and by his wounds we are healed.
ISAIAH 53:5, NIV

You are of God, little children, and have overcome them, because He who is in you is greater than he who is in the world.
1 JOHN 4:4, NKJV

Through the LORD's mercies we are not consumed, because His compassions fail not. They are new every morning; great is Your faithfulness.
LAMENTATIONS 3:22–23, NKJV

1 / Are you thinking thoughts of defeat, worry, lack, can't-do-it? Or are you thinking thoughts of victory, favor, healing, breakthroughs, abundance?

2 / What thoughts are stopping your success? What can you tell yourself instead?

3 / What are you thinking about your future?

4 / What's playing in your mind? Are there some tenants you need to evict? Are there destructive, discouraging thoughts that you need to stop allowing in?

5 / What negative thoughts are you evicting from your thoughts? What positive thoughts will replace them?

6 / Before you dwell on the negative, before you let it take root, ask yourself: *Where is this negative thought coming from?*

WHAT IS GOD SAYING TO YOU?

NOTES / MENTAL

NOTES / MENTAL

NOTES / MENTAL

PHYSICAL

2 Your Physical Strength

I praise you because
I am fearfully and
wonderfully made; your
works are wonderful,
I know that full well.

PSALM 139:14 / NIV

In today's hectic world, beneath people's packed calendars and long to-do lists, there's a truth hiding out. Too many people don't like themselves. In this section, get ready to discover how God looks at you and how you should see yourself.

Here, you'll gain a greater understanding of:

- **God's Love:** Know that God loves you for who you are, not for what you do. His love never changes.
- **Your Own Opinion:** It's important to think good things about yourself. Even if others doubt you, let your heart, filled with God's love, be the loudest voice.
- **Value from God:** Always remember your worth isn't determined by what others say but by what God believes about you.

Hold on to these truths. You aren't just another face in the crowd. You are crowned with glory and honor. See your true value through His loving eyes.

Too many people go around feeling wrong on the inside. They don't really like who they are. They think: "If I were just a little taller, if I had a better personality, if my metabolism was a little faster, if I just looked like him or her . . . then I would feel good about myself."

1 / GOD WENT TO GREAT LENGTHS TO MAKE YOU EXACTLY LIKE HE WANTED.

You didn't accidentally get your personality. You didn't just happen to get your height, your looks, your skin color, your gifts. He designed you on purpose to be the way you are. **You have what you need to fulfill your destiny.** If you needed to be taller, God would have made you taller. If you needed to be a different nationality God would have made you that way. If you needed to look like her instead of you, you would have looked like her. **You've got to be confident in who God made you to be.**

Ephesians 2:10 says that we are God's masterpiece.

- That means you are not ordinary.
- You didn't come off an assembly line.
- You weren't mass-produced.
- You are one of a kind.

Nobody in this world has your fingerprints. There will never be another you. If you're going to reach your highest potential, you have to see yourself as unique, as an original, as God's very own masterpiece.

> *Just as our bodies have many parts and each part has a special function, so it is with Christ's body. We are many parts of one body, and we all belong to each other.*
> Romans 12:4–5, NLT

2 / DO YOU KNOW WHO YOU ARE?

When I was in my early 20s, I was sitting on the beach in India all alone, watching the sunset. It was a magnificent scene. The water was so blue. As far as I could see from the right to the left, miles of beach and palm trees. The sun was huge on the horizon, just about to set. As I sat there reflecting, thinking about my life, I heard God ask me something — not out loud, but an impression down in my spirit. He said, "Joel, you think this is a beautiful picture, do you?" I said, "Yes, God. I think this is a magnificent picture." He said, "Well, what do you think would be My most prized painting? My most incredible creation?" I thought about it a moment. I said, "God, it must be this sunset. This is magnificent." He said, "No, it's not this." Earlier that year I had been in the Rocky Mountains. They were spectacular. I said, "God, I bet it's the Rocky Mountains." He said, "No, not that." I thought, "What could it be? The solar system? The Milky Way?" He said, "No. My most prized possession, the painting that I'm the proudest of is you." I thought, "Me? It couldn't be me. I'm ordinary. I'm just like everybody else." He said, "No. You don't understand. When I made the solar system, the waters, the mountains, I was proud of that. That was great. But, when I made you, I breathed my very life into you. I created you in My own image." Friend, **you** are God's most prized possession. Don't go around feeling wrong about yourself. Quit wishing you were taller, or had a better personality, or looked like somebody else. You've been painted by the most incredible Painter there could ever be.

3 / YOU ARE EXTREMELY VALUABLE.

When God created you, He stepped back, looked and said, "That was good. Another masterpiece."

> *So God created man in his own image, in the image of God he created him; male and female he created them. And God blessed them . . . And God saw everything that he had made, and behold, it was very good.* Genesis 1:27–28, 31, ESV

DO THIS
Look at yourself in the mirror and say: I am made in God's image. I am of great value.

He stamped His approval on you. You know how on the back of shirts most of the time there's a tag. It says, "Made in America. Made in China. Made in Mexico?" Well, somewhere on you there's a tag that says, "Made by Almighty God." Now put your shoulders back. Hold your head up high. You are extremely valuable.

> *"Look at the birds of the air; they do not sow or reap or store away in barns, and yet your heavenly Father feeds them. Are you not much more valuable than they?"*
> Matthew 6:26, NIV

You have royal blood flowing through your veins.

> *But you are a chosen race, a royal priesthood, a holy nation, a people for his own possession, that you may proclaim the excellencies of him who called you out of darkness into his marvelous light.* 1 Peter, 2:9, ESV

You are wearing a crown of favor.

> *You have made them a little lower than the angels and crowned them with glory and honor.* Psalm 8:5, NIV

When negative thoughts come, telling you everything that you're not, you need to remind yourself of this: "I've got the fingerprints of God all over me: the way I look, the way I smile, my gifts, my personality. I know I am not average. I am a masterpiece." Those are the thoughts that should be playing in your mind all day long.

4 / DWELL ON WHAT GOD SAYS ABOUT YOU.

God does not make anything average! If you have breath to breathe, you are a masterpiece. Now people may try to make you feel average. Your own thoughts may try to convince you that you are ordinary. Life will try to push you down and steal your sense of value. That's why all through the day you have to remind yourself who your Painter is. When you dwell on the fact that Almighty God breathed His life into you, He approved you, equipped you, empowered you, then any thoughts of low self-esteem, inferiority won't have a chance.

> *Do you not know that you are God's temple and that God's Spirit dwells in you?* 1 Corinthians 3:16, ESV

5 / YOUR WORTH COMES FROM YOUR CREATOR.

A few years ago, I was in somebody's home. They have all these paintings on the wall. And to me they weren't very impressive. In fact, some of them looked like they had been painted by a child, very abstract, modern, paint thrown here and there. But later that evening they mentioned how they had paid over a million dollars for just one of those paintings. I looked at it again and thought, "Wow! That is beautiful, isn't it?" Come to find out, it was an original painting by the famous artist Pablo Picasso. What dawned on me that night is, it's not so much what the painting looks like. It's who the painter is. The painting gets its value from its creator. In the same way, our value doesn't come because of what we look like, or what we do, or who we know. Our value comes from the fact that Almighty God is our Painter. Now don't criticize what God has painted.

- Accept yourself.
- Approve yourself.
- You are not an accident.

You have been fearfully and wonderfully made.

> *I praise you, for I am fearfully and wonderfully made.*
> *Wonderful are your works; my soul knows it very well.*
> Psalm 139:14, ESV

PHYSICAL

"Friend, *you* are one of God's most prized creations."
—Joel

6 / "GOOD MORNING, YOU WONDERFUL THING!"

I wonder what would happen if all through the day, instead of putting ourselves down, instead of dwelling on the negative, we would go around thinking, "I'm a masterpiece. I'm wonderfully made. I'm talented. I'm original. I have everything that I need." See, the enemy doesn't want you to feel good about yourself. He would love for you to go through life listening to the nagging voices reminding you of everything that you are not. I dare you to get up each day and say, "Good morning, you wonderful thing! You are fearfully and wonderfully made." That's what David said in Psalm 139:14, "God, I praise You because You have made me in an amazing way. What You have done is wonderful." How many of us will be bold enough to say like David, "I'm amazing. I'm a masterpiece." For most people, those thoughts never enter into their minds. They're too busy putting themselves down, focusing on their flaws, comparing themselves to others who they think are better. No, your Painter, your Creator says about you: "You're amazing. You're wonderful. You're a masterpiece." Now it's up to you to get in agreement with God. If you go around focused on your flaws, listening to what other people are saying, you can miss your destiny. The recording that should be playing in our mind all day long is, "I'm valuable. I'm a masterpiece. I'm a child of the Most High God." This may be what's holding you back. Your recording is negative. There are enough people in life already against you. Don't be against yourself. Change your recording. Start seeing yourself as the masterpiece God created you to be.

DO THIS
Put up notes on your mirror as a daily reminder: You are amazing. You are wonderful. You are a masterpiece.

> *"Before I shaped you in the womb, I knew all about you.*
> *Before you saw the light of day, I had holy plans for you . . ."*
> Jeremiah 1:5, MSG

7 / REALIZE YOUR WORTH.

I read a story about a man who died in extreme poverty. At one point, he was homeless, living on the streets, barely getting by in life. After the funeral, some of his relatives went to his rundown apartment and gathered up his belongings. He had a painting on the wall. They took it down and sold it at a garage sale. The person that bought it took the painting to a local art gallery to learn more about it. Well, it was extremely valuable. It had been painted in the 1800s by a famous artist. It ended up selling at auction for over $3 million. That man lived his whole life in poverty because he didn't realize what he had! In the same way, you have been painted by the most famous artist there could ever be. But if you don't understand your value, you'll go around thinking, "Well, I'm just kind of average. I'm not that talented. I've made a lot of mistakes in life." If you let that negative recording play, just like this man, even though you have everything you need, even though you're full of potential, you'll never tap into it. That's why every morning you need to remind yourself, "I am not average. I am not ordinary. I have the fingerprints of God all over me. I am a masterpiece."

> *"For I know the plans I have for you, declares the LORD, plans*
> *for welfare and not for evil, to give you a future and a hope."*
> Jeremiah 29:11, ESV

8 / YOU HAVE A $6 MILLION BODY.

There was an article in a medical magazine. It talked about how researchers scientifically calculated how much money the human body is worth. They added up the cost of all the enzymes, cells, tissue, organs, and hormones — contained in the body. They concluded that an average-sized person is worth $6 million. Maybe you've heard of "The Six Million Dollar Man?" You can put your shoulders back. You can have a spring in your step. Your Heavenly Father has invested $6 million in you. The good news is you didn't even have to pay taxes on it.

> *But by the grace of God I am what I am, and His grace toward me was not in vain; but I labored more abundantly than they all, yet not I, but the grace of God which was with me.*
> 1 Corinthians 15:10, NKJV

9 / YOUR OPINION OF YOURSELF IS THE MOST IMPORTANT OPINION.

Jesus said to love your neighbor as you love yourself. If you don't love yourself in a healthy way, you will never be able to love others in the way you should.

> *Jesus replied: "'Love the Lord your God with all your heart and with all your soul and with all your mind.' This is the first and greatest commandment. And the second is like it: 'Love*

your neighbor as yourself.' All the Law and the Prophets hang on these two commandments." Matthew 22:37–40, NIV

This is why some people don't have good relationships. If you don't get along with yourself, you'll never get along with others. We all have weaknesses, shortcomings, things that we wish were different. But God never designed us to go through life being against ourselves. The opinion you have of yourself is the most important opinion that you have. If you see yourself as less than, not talented, not valuable, then you will become exactly that. You are constantly conveying what you feel on the inside. Even subconsciously, you're sending messages out. If you feel unattractive on the inside, you can be the most beautiful person in the world, but you will convey feelings of unattractiveness. That's going to push people away. The problem is on the inside. **You carry yourself the way you see yourself.** I've seen just the opposite happen. A few years ago, I met a young lady and, on the surface, in the natural — and I say this very respectfully — she didn't have a lot of natural beauty (by the world's standards of beauty). But can I tell you? On the inside, she had it going on! She knew she was made in the image of Almighty God. She knew she was crowned with favor. She may have looked ordinary, but she thought extraordinary. She carried herself like a queen. She walked like she was royalty. She smiled like she was Miss America. She dressed like she was headed for the runway. She may have bought it at a secondhand store, but she wore it like it was brand new. All I could say was, "You go, girl!"

DO THIS
Imagine confidence like a coat you put on yourself as you get ready for the day. You wear it well.

"For I know the plans I have for you, declares the Lord, plans for welfare and not for evil, to give you a future and a hope."

JEREMIAH 29:11 / ESV

What was the difference? On the inside, she sees herself as beautiful, strong, talented, valuable. What's on the inside will eventually show up on the outside. Because she sees herself as a masterpiece, she exudes strength, beauty, confidence. Here's a key: people see you the way you see yourself. If you see yourself as strong, talented, valuable, "with it," that's the way other people will see you. Those are the messages you're sending out. But if you see yourself as less than, not talented, not valuable, that's the way others will see you.

If some of you would change the opinion you have of yourself, if you would quit focusing on your flaws and everything you wish was different, if you would quit comparing yourself to somebody else that you think is better and start loving yourself in a healthy way, being proud of who God made you to be, then as you send out these different messages, it's going to bring new opportunities, new relationships, new levels of God's favor. This is what the Israelites did. In Scripture, when 10 of the spies came back from the Promised Land and they had seen how huge their opponents were, they said to Moses, "We were in our own sights as grasshoppers, and so we were in their sights." Notice they didn't say, "Moses, those people insulted us. They called us grasshoppers." No, they went in with a grasshopper mentality. They said, "We were in our own sights as grasshoppers." That's what they conveyed. Here's the principle at work: "And so we were in their sights." In other words, "They saw us the way we saw ourselves." If you put off feelings of inferiority, people will treat you as inferior. You may feel like you have a disadvantage like the Israelites. You don't have the size, the talent, the education. That's all right. All that matters is Almighty God breathed His life into you. He created you as a person of destiny. He put seeds of greatness on the inside. Now do your part. Start seeing yourself as the masterpiece God created you to be.

10 / YOU ARE CROWNED WITH HONOR.

The Scripture talks about how God has made us to be kings and priests unto Him. Men, you need to start seeing yourself as a king. Women, start seeing yourself as a queen. Start carrying yourself like royalty. Not in arrogance, thinking that you're better than others. I'm talking about humility. Be proud of who God made you to be. You are not better than anyone else, but can I tell you? You are not less than anyone else, either. It doesn't matter how many degrees they have. It doesn't matter how important of a family they come from. No, understand, your Father created the whole universe. When He breathed His life into you and sent you to planet Earth, you didn't come as ordinary. You didn't come as average. He put a crown of honor on your head. Now start thinking like royalty, talking like royalty, dressing like royalty, walking like royalty, acting like royalty.

> *"Since you are precious and honored in my sight, and because I love you, I will give people in exchange for you, nations in exchange for your life."* Isaiah 43:4, NIV

I was in England a few years ago. They were having a ceremony to honor the Queen. When the Queen walked in the room, you could feel the strength, the confidence, the dignity. She had her head held high, a pleasant smile on her face. She waved at everyone like they were her best friend. What's interesting is there were all kinds of important people in that room. There were presidents of other nations, world-renowned entertainers, famous athletes, scientists, some of the brightest, most talented people in the world. But by the way the Queen carried herself you would have thought she was the cat's meow. She had it going on: strong, confident, secure. The Queen wasn't the wealthiest woman in the room. She wasn't the fittest or the most educated. A lot of people would have been intimidated walking into that room, but not her. She walked in like she owned the place. Why? She knew who she was. She was the Queen. She came from a long line of royalty. It was engrained in her thinking, "I'm not average. I'm not ordinary. I am one of a kind." No doubt some mornings when the Queen woke up, the same thoughts came to her mind that come to all of us. "You're not as beautiful as your sister. You're not as talented as your brother. You're not as smart as your coworker. Be intimidated. You're inferior." The Queen let that go in one ear and out the other. She thought, "What are you talking about? It doesn't matter how I compare to others. I'm the Queen. I've got royalty in my blood. In my DNA is generations of influence, honor, prestige."

If you and I could ever just start seeing ourselves as the kings, the queens, that God made us to be, we would never be intimidated again. You don't have to be the most talented to feel good about yourself. You don't have to have the most education, the most success. When you understand your Heavenly Father breathed His life into you, you will understand that you, too, come from a long line of royalty. Instead

DO THIS
What is the confident posture of a royal? As a son or daughter of the King, put your shoulders back and hold your head high today!

of being intimidated or insecure by someone that you think is more important, you can do like the Queen. Just be at ease, be kind, be confident, be friendly, knowing that you are one of a kind. Ladies, you may not be the most beautiful person, but be confident you're a queen.

Men, you may not be the most successful but stand up tall. You're a king. Not crowned by people but crowned by Almighty God. But a lot of times we think, "Well, Joel. I can't feel good about myself. I've got this addiction. I struggle with a bad temper. I've made a lot of mistakes in life. I sure don't feel like a masterpiece." Here's the key. Your value is not based on your performance. You don't have to do enough good and then maybe God will approve you. God has already approved you.

> "You will keep in perfect and constant peace the one whose mind is steadfast [that is, committed and focused on You — in both inclination and character], because he trusts and takes refuge in You [with hope and confident expectation]"
> Isaiah 62:3, AMP

11 / GOD LOVES YOU FOR WHO YOU ARE, NOT FOR WHAT YOU'VE DONE.

When Jesus was being baptized by John in the Jordan River, He hadn't started His ministry yet. He had never opened one blind eye, never raised the dead, never turned water into wine. He had not performed one miracle. But a voice boomed out of the heavens.

"This is my Son, whom I love; with him I am well pleased."
Matthew 3:17, NIV

His Father was pleased with Him because of who He was, not because of anything He had done or not done. We think, "Well, if I could break this addiction, then I'd feel good about myself. If I could read my Bible more, if I bite my tongue and not argue so much, then maybe I wouldn't be against myself." No, you've got to learn to accept yourself while you're in the process of changing. We all have areas we need to improve, but we're not supposed to go around down on ourselves because we haven't arrived. When you're against yourself it doesn't help you to do better. It makes you do worse. You may have a bad habit you know you need to overcome but if you go around guilty, condemned, thinking about all the times you fail, the times you've blown it, that will not motivate you to go forward. That's going to cause you to do worse. You've got to shake off the guilt. Shake off the condemnation. You may not be where you want to be but you can look back and thank God you're not where you used to be. You're growing. You're making progress. Now do yourself a big favor and quit listening to the accusing voices. That's the enemy trying to convince you to be against yourself. He knows if you don't like yourself, you will never become what God created you to be.

In Genesis 1, we read how God had just created the Heavens, the earth, the sea, the animals and Adam and Eve. Verse 31 says, *God looked over all he had made, and he saw that it was very good!* (NLT). When God looks at you, He says, "You are excellent in every way." "Well, not me,

Joel. I've got these bad habits. I've got some shortcomings. I've made some mistakes in the past." No, get out of that defeated mentality. You may not be perfect, but God is not basing your value on your performance. He's looking at your heart. He is looking at the fact that you're trying. You wouldn't be here if you didn't have a heart to please God. Now quit being down on yourself. Quit living condemned and dare to believe you are excellent in every way. Our attitude should be, "Yes, I may make some mistakes. I may have some flaws and weaknesses, but I am not going to live my life guilty, condemned. I know God has already approved me. I am excellent in every way. I am His masterpiece." If you're going to overcome in those areas, you have to not only stay positive toward yourself, but you also have to be bold enough to celebrate who God made you to be. Be proud of who you are. I know people, they're good at celebrating others. They'll compliment their friends. They'll brag on others. And that's good. We should celebrate other people, but make sure you also celebrate yourself. **You are smart. You are talented. You are beautiful. There is something special about you.** You can't get so caught up in celebrating others, putting them on a high pedestal, to where you think, "They are so great, and I am so average. She is so beautiful, and I am so plain." No, they may have more natural beauty, more talent in some area, but let me tell you, God didn't leave anybody out. You have something that they don't have. You're good at something that they're not good at. And it's fine to celebrate them and say, "Wow! Look how great they are," as long as you follow it up by saying internally, "And you know what? I'm great too. I'm smart too. I'm talented, too."

PHYSICAL

"You carry yourself the way you see yourself."
—Joel

No one ever hated their own body, but they feed and care for their body, just as Christ does the church — for we are members of his body. Ephesians 5:29–30, NIV

12 / SEE YOURSELF AS A MASTERPIECE OF ALMIGHTY GOD.

It's like this man I heard about. He was the mayor of a small town. He was in a parade riding in a float down Main Street with his wife next to him. While he was waving at all the different people, he spotted his wife's former boyfriend in the crowd. He owned and ran the local gas station. He whispered to his wife, "Aren't you glad you didn't marry him? You'd be working at a gas station." She whispered back, "No. If I would've married him, he'd be the mayor." See, you've got to know who you are. God breathed His life into you. You have royalty in your blood. You are excellent in every way. Now put your shoulders back. Hold your head up high. Start carrying yourself like royalty. You are not average. You are not ordinary. You are a masterpiece. Get up every morning and remind yourself who your Painter is. Your value doesn't come because of who you are. It comes because of whose you are.

> *The Spirit himself bears witness with our spirit that we are children of God.* Romans 8:16, ESV

Remember, the most important opinion you have is the opinion of yourself. How you see yourself is how other people are going to see you. I'm asking you today to see yourself as a king. See yourself as a queen. Not arrogantly but in humility. Now some of you need to change the recording that's playing in your mind from, "I'm slow. I'm unattractive. I'm nothing special." to say like David, "I'm amazing. I'm a masterpiece. I'm talented. I am one of a kind." If you will see yourself as the masterpiece God created you to be, then you will go through life confident, secure. Your gifts and talents will come out to the full. The right people will be drawn to you. And I believe and declare you will overcome every obstacle, defeat every enemy. You will become everything God has created you to be. In Jesus' name.

YOUR PHYSICAL STRENGTH, GOD'S MASTERPIECE

Just as our bodies have many parts and each part has a special function, so it is with Christ's body. We are many parts of one body, and we all belong to each other.
ROMANS 12:4–5, NLT

So God created man in his own image, in the image of God he created him; male and female he created them. And God blessed them... And God saw everything that he had made, and behold, it was very good.
GENESIS 1:27–28, 31, ESV

"Look at the birds of the air; they do not sow or reap or store away in barns, and yet your heavenly Father feeds them. Are you not much more valuable than they?"
MATTHEW 6:26, NIV

But you are a chosen race, a royal priesthood, a holy nation, a people for his own possession, that you may proclaim the excellencies of him who called you out of darkness into his marvelous light.
1 PETER 2:9, ESV

You have made them a little lower than the angels and crowned them with glory and honor.
PSALM 8:5, NIV

Do you not know that you are God's temple and that God's Spirit dwells in You?
1 CORINTHIANS 3:16, ESV

I praise you, for I am fearfully and wonderfully made. Wonderful are your works; my soul knows it very well.
PSALM 139:14, ESV

"Before I shaped you in the womb, I knew all about you. Before you saw the light of day, I had holy plans for you . . ."
JEREMIAH 1:5, MSG

"For I know the plans I have for you, declares the LORD, plans for welfare and not for evil, to give you a future and a hope."
JEREMIAH 29:11, ESV

But by the grace of God, I am what I am . . .
1 CORINTHIANS 15:10, KJV

"Since you are precious and honored in my sight, and because I love you, I will give people in exchange for you, nations in exchange for your life."
ISAIAH 43:4, NIV

Jesus replied: "'Love the Lord your God with all your heart and with all your soul and with all your mind.' This is the first and greatest commandment. And the second is like it: 'Love your neighbor as yourself.' All the Law and the Prophets hang on these two commandments."
MATTHEW 22:37–40, NIV

You will also be [considered] a crown of glory and splendor in the hand of the LORD, and a royal diadem [exceedingly beautiful] in the hand of your God.
ISAIAH 62:3, AMP

And a voice from heaven said, "This is my Son, whom I love; with him I am well pleased."
MATTHEW 3:17, NIV

No one ever hated their own body, but they feed and care for their body, just as Christ does the church — for we are members of his body.
EPHESIANS 5:29–30, NIV

The Spirit himself bears witness with our spirit that we are children of God.
ROMANS 8:16, ESV

PROMISES / PHYSICAL

1 / How do you see yourself? Are you living as the person of destiny that God created you to be? If not, start to consciously change those negative thoughts into what God says about you and see how your life will change!

2 / Have you ever come across something of value where you least expected it? How did you feel? What did you do? Now think about yourself being that valuable find. How does this change your views about your physical self?

3 / Think about a situation where you compare yourself to others. Maybe at work, at school, at the mall or store. What can you tell yourself now when those thoughts come to mind?

4 / Recall a time in your life when God's Word changed how you viewed your physical self. What shifted in your thoughts or prayers?

5 / How has God "spoken" to you? What did He convey? In what way(s) did His message change your life?

6 / Have you ever wanted to change something about yourself? What was it and why? What's stopping you from trusting what God says about you?

REFLECTION / PHYSICAL

WHAT IS GOD SAYING TO YOU?

NOTES / PHYSICAL

NOTES / PHYSICAL

NOTES / PHYSICAL

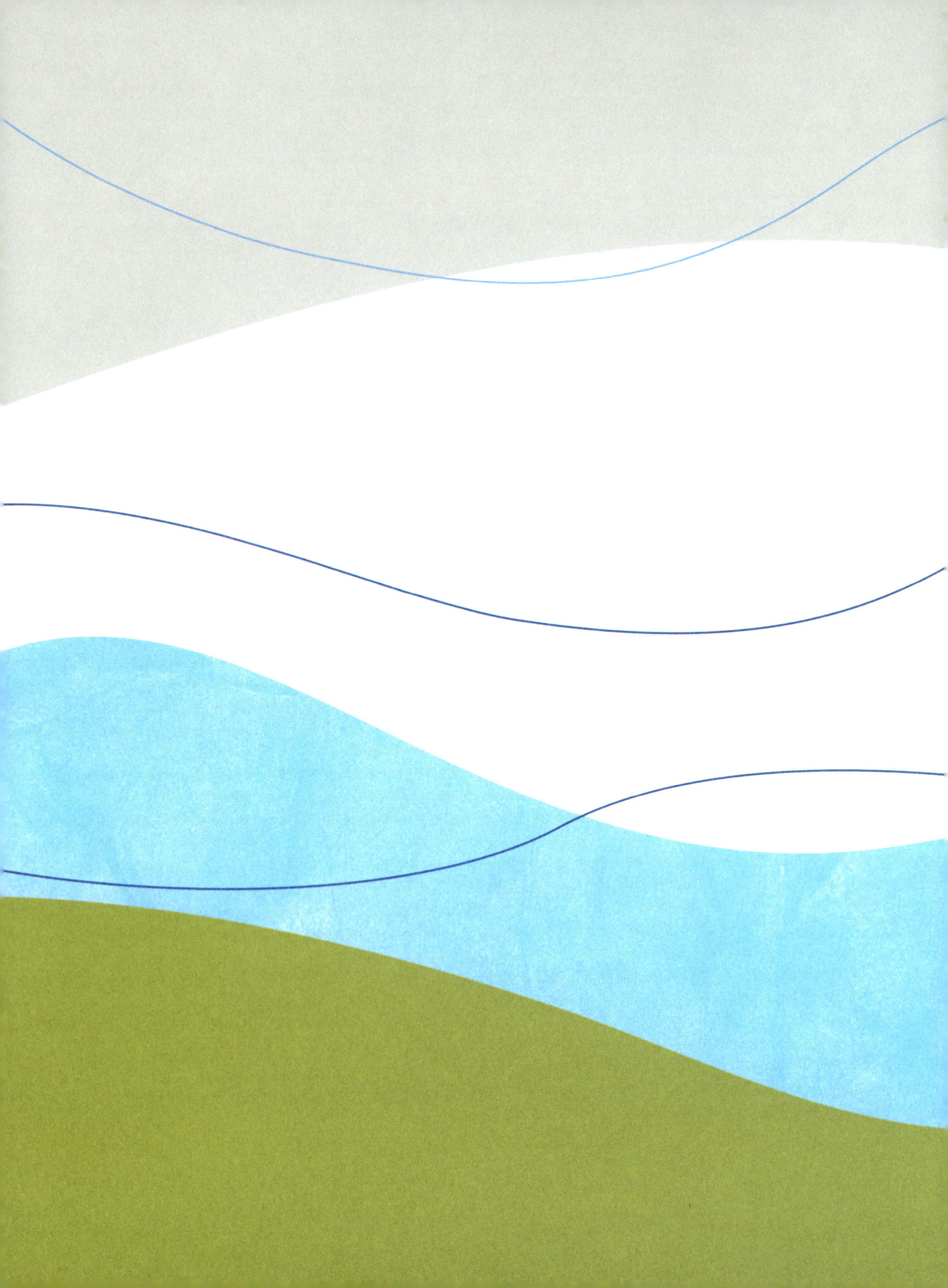

3 Your Spiritual Strength

SPIRITUAL

For we live by faith, not by sight.

2 CORINTHIANS 5:7 / NIV

You may have heard me say, "You're not an accident. You have a destiny, a purpose, a God-given calling on your life." At the core of this purpose is your spirit. It's the essence of who you are. It was part of you before you were born, and it goes far beyond the body or mind. It's the divine spark, the very breath of God in you. My heart for you in this section is that you will discover deeper truths about these points (and so many more):

- **The Divine Connection:** Understand the supernatural connection you share with the Creator.
- **Spirit over Matter:** Realize the power of your spirit over challenges and adversities.
- **Nurture Your Spirit:** Receive encouraging insights to help you lean in to God.

You're more than your circumstances, more than your past, more than the challenges that confront you. Your spirit, given by God, is the true reflection of who you are. As you read this section, I believe and declare that you will hear that still, small voice down in your spirit. I pray that your spiritual ears and eyes are open, sensitive, and responsive. And that with His guidance, you will fulfill His plan for your life! Let's get started!

Did you know that God has given you "spiritual ears"? It's true. Just as you have physical ears, you also have spiritual ears. That's because God doesn't speak to you out loud, like you see in the movies, He speaks to you in your spirit. And many times, God will speak things to your spirit that contradict what you can see with your eyes. If you're struggling in your finances, you can't seem to get ahead, you'll hear that voice saying, **"You're blessed. You're prosperous. You have more than enough."** If your children are off course, not making good decisions, that voice will tell you, **"Your children are mighty in the land, your seed is blessed, they will fulfill their destiny."** If you're fighting a sickness, it doesn't look like you'll ever get well, you'll hear a voice saying, **"You're healthy, you're whole."** It's just the opposite of what it looks like. Why?

1 / GOD CALLS YOU WHAT YOU ARE BEFORE IT HAPPENS.

When you're sick, God calls you well. When you're addicted, God calls you free. When you're not able to conceive, God calls you a mother. Abraham didn't have any children, and God called him a father of many nations.

> "I have made you the father of many nations" — in the presence of the God in whom he believed, who gives life to the dead and calls into existence the things that do not exist.
> Romans 4:17, ESV

Gideon was insecure and afraid. He told God, "I can't lead the Israelites. I come from the poorest family." He saw himself as weak, unqualified. But God called him a mighty hero.

2 / YOU'LL HEAR THINGS IN YOUR SPIRIT THAT DON'T MAKE SENSE TO YOUR MIND.

You may think, "Joel, I'm not free, I still have this addiction. I'm not blessed, I have all these problems." Gideon said to God, "I'm not a mighty hero. I'm the least one in my father's house." Abraham said, in effect, "I'm not a father of many nations. I don't have one child." If you're going to see it come to pass, you have to believe what you hear in your spirit and not what you see with your eyes.

For we live by faith, not by sight. 2 Corinthians 5:7, NIV

People may tell you that you'll never get well, circumstances may look like you'll never get out of debt, never meet the right person, never accomplish your dreams.

But if you listen, you'll hear a voice saying, "Healing is coming, you will lend and not borrow, new doors are about to open." Don't let what you see talk you out of what you've heard with your spiritual ears.

God is saying to you what He said to Gideon,

"You are a mighty hero. You're going to accomplish big things. You're going to go further than you can imagine."

> *The angel of the LORD appeared to him and said, "Mighty hero, the LORD is with you!"* Judges 6:12, NLT

He's saying what He said to Abraham, "You're going to have those children, you're going to conceive, your baby is on the way."

He's saying to you what He said to David, "You're going to defeat that giant. Yes, that obstacle is big, but you have greatness in you. You are anointed, equipped, empowered."

> *Now may the God of peace who brought again from the dead our Lord Jesus, the great shepherd of the sheep, by the blood of the eternal covenant, equip you with everything good that you may do his will, working in us that which is pleasing in his sight, through Jesus Christ, to whom be glory forever and ever. Amen.* Hebrews 13:20–21, ESV

DO THIS
Write down what you hear in your spirit. Journal those things you don't see in the natural yet.

He is saying to you what He said to my mother, "That cancer is not the end. The sickness is not your final chapter. Restoration is coming. Things are about to turn in your favor." Quit being discouraged by what you see, and start being encouraged by what you hear in your spirit. The Scripture says the things we see are only temporary, but what we hear, what God speaks to us, that's permanent. We fix our attention, not on things that are seen, but on things that are unseen.

> *What can be seen lasts only for a time, but what cannot be seen lasts forever.* 2 Corinthians 4:18, GNT

3 / IT'S SUBJECT TO CHANGE.

That sickness may look permanent, but the truth is, **it is subject to change.** One touch of God's favor, and you'll be well. That addiction you've had for years. It looks like that's your destiny. **Don't believe that lie. It is subject to change.** You may feel like you're stuck. You're not seeing any good breaks, not seeing any growth. Stay in faith. It is subject to change. **God has the final say!** He said the path of the righteous — your path — gets brighter and brighter.

> *But the path of the just (righteous) is like the light of dawn, that shines brighter and brighter until [it reaches its full strength and glory in] the perfect day.* Proverbs 4:18, AMP

If you'll listen down in your spirit, you'll hear that voice saying, "New levels are coming, new opportunities, new relationships, favor is in your future." **In 1 Kings 18, there was a great drought in the land.** It hadn't rained for three and a half years. The crops had dried up, the food supply was limited. People were worried, they didn't know what they were going to do. The prophet Elijah came along and told the King, *"There is the sound of abundance of rain"* (v. 41, NKJV). There wasn't a cloud in the sky. Everywhere he looked it was dry, barren, dead trees, no vegetation. It had been that way for years. I'm sure the King thought, "Elijah, this heat is getting to you. You're hearing things. There's no thunder. There's no sound of an abundance of rain. It's just like it's always been."

That's the way God is:

- When you're in a drought, God will talk to you about rain.
- When you're in lack, He'll talk to you about abundance.
- When you feel insignificant, He'll talk to you about greatness.
- When you're lonely, God will talk to you about a great relationship.

4 / GOD SPEAKS TO YOUR SPIRIT ABOUT WHAT'S COMING.

- It may be the opposite of what your circumstances look like.
- You heard abundance but all you can see is lack.
- You heard healing but all you can see is sickness.

You heard new levels but all you can see is more of the same. The question is: Whose report are you going to believe? What you see with your eyes or what you hear down in your spirit — is it the report of the Lord? Like Elijah, I hear the sound of healing, the sound of freedom, the sound of breakthroughs, the sound of new levels, I hear the sound of abundance.

God is about to do a new thing. He's about to exceed your expectations.

> *"Forget the former things; do not dwell on the past. See, I am doing a new thing! Now it springs up; do you not perceive it? I am making a way in the wilderness and streams in the wasteland."* Isaiah 43:18–19, NIV

SPIRITUAL

"Quit being discouraged by what you see, and start being encouraged by what you hear."
–Joel

You may not see any sign of it. Everything looks the same, but get ready. The rain is coming.

5 / WHAT YOU HEARD IS ON THE WAY.

"Joel, I heard in my spirit that I would start my own business, but all I can see is this job I'm working at. I must not have heard right." Stay in faith, it's coming. Your circumstances may say, "You've reached your limits. You can't go any further. Just settle where you are." That's one report. But if you believe that, you'll get stuck. If you'll tune that out and believe the report of the Lord, if you'll believe what you hear in your spirit, then it will override what you hear in the natural. **When you get in agreement with God, then you will become what He says about you. You will have what He says you'll have.** Maybe you're dealing with an illness. But the Bible says, "By His stripes you are healed." Believe the report of the Lord and that healing is coming.

> But He was wounded for our transgressions, He was bruised for our iniquities; the chastisement for our peace was upon Him, and by His stripes we are healed. Isaiah 53:5, NKJV

You're struggling in your career. God says you will lend and not borrow. Believe His report. An increase is coming. You're fighting an addiction.

DO THIS
Begin speaking out loud those things that you don't see yet. Tell yourself and tell others.

God says,

> *"Therefore if the Son makes you free, you shall be free indeed."*
> John 8:36, NKJV

Believe the report that freedom is coming. What you hear will override what you see. When Elijah heard the sound of an abundance of rain, they had been in the drought for years, no sign of rain. He could have thought, "I'm keeping this to myself. I'm not going to tell anyone what I heard. They'll think I'm crazy." But Elijah was bold enough to announce what he heard. He went right to the king and said, "I hear the sound of an abundance of rain."

6 / IT'S NOT ENOUGH TO JUST BELIEVE WHAT YOU HEARD. YOU NEED TO ANNOUNCE IT.

When you're fighting a sickness, tell someone,

- "I am healthy."
- "I am whole."
- "I will live and not die."

They may look at you and say, "What do you mean? You saw the medical report. There's no sign of you getting well."

When you announce it, it sets the miracle in motion.

Your words have creative power.
You give life to your faith by speaking it out.

The scripture says,

*Oh, give thanks to the Lord, for He is good! for His mercy endures forever. Let the redeemed of the Lord **say so**, whom He has redeemed from the hand of the enemy.* Psalm 107:1–2, NKJV

If you want to break the addiction, say so! If you want to start that business, say so! If you want to accomplish your dream, say so! There may not be any sign of it. But like Elijah, you need to announce to people:

- I am blessed.
- I am free.
- I am going to start my business.
- We're going to have a baby.
- We're going to move into a new house.
- Our son is going to do great things.

You may hear people say, "Are you sure? I thought your son was running with the wrong crowd. Hasn't he been off course, getting into trouble?" You declare, "Yes, but that's temporary. That's subject to change. That's what you see with your eyes but what I heard in my spirit is, *"as for me and my house, we will serve the Lord."*

". . . But as for me and my house, we will serve the LORD."
Joshua 24:15, NKJV

If you'll start announcing what you've heard, not in arrogance, not like a know-it-all, but in humility, with a quiet confidence, then you're releasing your faith.

7 / ANNOUNCING WHAT YOU HEARD IS WHAT ALLOWS GOD TO BRING IT TO PASS.

I have these friends that tried to get pregnant for years with no success. They went through all the fertility treatments, did everything they could. Finally, the doctor said there was no chance she could get pregnant. She was getting up there in years, and I thought they had accepted that it wasn't going to work out that way.

Maybe they would adopt or try another option.

But this lady never changed her mind. She worked in our children's department. She was constantly telling us, "When I have my baby." Not "if" but "when."

She acted like there was no doubt, like it was already on the calendar.

Now, I like to think of myself as a person of faith, somebody that will believe with you, but even I thought, "You're getting too old. It's not going to be possible." **Just because people don't believe, it doesn't mean it's not going to happen.**

". . . But as for me and my house, we will serve the Lord."

JOSHUA 24:15 / NKJV

- The experts may say there's no way.
- Banks say you're not qualified.
- Friends say you'll never get that house.
- Coworkers say you could never start your business.

Like Elijah, there may not be a cloud in the sky, and yet you have the boldness to tell people that it's not just going to rain but there's going to be an abundance of rain! Don't be surprised if you have some naysayers. That's ok. Here's what I want you to see . . . You're not announcing it to get people to agree with you. You're not saying it out loud, so they will encourage you: "Yes, let me believe with you." Of course, that's great when it happens, but that's not the primary reason.

You're announcing it to show God that you believe what you heard. And you're announcing it to show the enemy that all the forces of darkness are not going to talk you out of what God put in your heart.

The enemy can't read your thoughts. He's not like God. God knows our thoughts before we think them, our words before we speak them. God is all-knowing. The enemy only knows what he hears you saying. Be careful what you let come out of your mouth. "I've had this sickness so long; I don't think I'll ever get well. I'll never accomplish my dreams. I'll always struggle with this addiction. This drought will never end." You're giving the enemy way too much information. That's showing your weaknesses, your doubts, your fears. But when he hears you saying, "I am strong. I am healthy. I am blessed. I hear the sound of abundance, the sound of healing, the sound of promotion."

All the enemy knows is that you are headed up. He cannot keep you from what God has in store.

Twenty years later, the doctor said to this lady, "You are pregnant, with not one child but with twins!" Today, she has two healthy children. I wonder what would have happened if she had not announced it. If she would have kept it to herself and thought, "I'm too old. I missed my chance." She wouldn't have seen those twins.

When you hear yourself saying, I will:
 . . . Have children.
 . . . Start my business.
 . . . See my family restored.

Those words go down in your own spirit and help you to stay in faith. But if all you hear is how bad the drought is and how it will never rain, those negative reports are going to keep you from the abundance that belongs to you. You need to start not only announcing what God put in your spirit but also do this:

8 / START THANKING HIM FOR WHAT YOU HEARD.

"Father, thank You that I'll have my baby! Thank You that I'm coming out of debt! Thank You that I'm free from this addiction! Thank You that new doors are opening in my career."

> *For we walk by faith, not by sight.*
> 2 Corinthians 5:7, ESV

Elijah was on top of Mount Carmel. He told his assistant to go look on the other side of the mountain and see if there was any sign of rain. The young man came back and said, "Elijah, there's not a cloud in the sky. It's perfectly clear. It's not going to rain." Elijah didn't get discouraged. He didn't think, "God, I must have heard You wrong." His attitude was, "I'm not moved by what you see. I know what I've heard." When you know what you've heard, you won't be upset when circumstances don't line up. You won't be discouraged because the medical report is not good. You won't give up on a dream because you've had setbacks. *Like Elijah, you're not moved by what you see.* You know what God has spoken to you! You've heard He is restoring health back unto you. You've heard that whatever you touch will prosper and succeed. You've heard that your spouse is on the way, favor is on the way, the rain is on the way!

DO THIS
What do you need to thank God for in advance? You can express your gratitude today.

9 / KNOW THE REAL BATTLE.

Maybe you're in a drought, it feels barren, things haven't worked out, you can hear rain in your spirit but there are no signs of it happening. It's been this way a long time. Can I tell you? This is the real battle. Are you going to let what you see talk you out of what you've heard God say to your spirit? No. Are you going to let the circumstances, what people say, or what hasn't worked out convince you to settle where you are, to give up on what you're believing for? **No, get your passion back!** God didn't create you to live in a drought, constantly struggling, stuck at one level. That's not your destiny, that's temporary. **Abundance** is coming. **Promotion** is coming. **Healing** is coming. **What you heard is on the way!**

I can imagine the young man thought, "Elijah must have missed it this time. He's performed a lot of miracles, but there's no rain coming. It's as clear as can be." I love what Elijah did. The young man said it wasn't going to happen. But instead of accepting it, Elijah sent him back to look again. Every time he came back and said, "Still nothing, it's not going to rain." He had him go back and look again and again and again. On the seventh time the young man came back and said, "This time I saw a small cloud starting to form." Elijah was so convinced it was going to happen that instead of changing his mind, instead of being talked out of it, *Elijah sent the young man back until that young man changed his mind!*

DO THIS
Take inventory of the people you allow to speak into your situation. Ask God to reveal those that will be in agreement with you and stand in faith.

10 / INSTEAD OF YOU CHANGING YOUR MIND, TELL OTHERS TO GO BACK AND LOOK AGAIN.

God will speak things to your spirit that contradict what you see with your eyes. Don't let people talk you out of what you heard. Instead of you changing your mind, tell them to go back and look again. At some point, they're going to see what God has spoken to you.

The people close to you, those you allow in your inner circle, they need to be in agreement with you. You can't afford to have doubters and naysayers constantly telling you that you can't accomplish your dreams. That you won't get well, and the problem is too big. Your destiny is too important to try to convince people what you heard, try to talk them into supporting you.

> *Now faith is the substance of things hoped for,*
> *the evidence of things not seen.* Hebrews 11:1, NKJV

Elijah didn't debate with the young man. He didn't try to persuade him. He kept sending him away until he believed. If you're going to stay in faith, you may have to send some people away for a little while. You may have to change who you eat lunch with at the office. You may have to distance yourself from that relative who tells you what you can't become.

This is what my father did. He grew up very poor. His parents were cotton farmers. They lost everything during the Great Depression. They barely had enough food. My father had to put cardboard in the bottom of his shoes to cover up the holes. He dropped out of high school. He had no future to speak of, no sense of purpose. But at seventeen years old, he gave his life to Christ, the first one in his family. God put a dream in his heart to become a pastor. He believed that somehow, he could touch the world. He told his parents he was going to leave the farm and go out and minister. His parents were good people, but their vision was limited. They said, "John, you'd better stay here on the farm with us. All you know how to do is pick cotton. You're going to get out there and fail." If my father would have taken their advice, he would have missed his destiny.

> *The LORD will fulfill his purpose for me; your steadfast love, O LORD, endures forever. Do not forsake the work of your hands.*
> Psalm 138:8, ESV

He knew what he heard. The problem was that the people closest to him couldn't see it. He loved his family. He was always respectful, but he didn't let people talk him out of what he heard. GOD WILL PUT THINGS IN YOUR SPIRIT THAT SEEM BIGGER THAN YOU CAN ACCOMPLISH, THAT DON'T SEEM POSSIBLE. You don't have the talent, the resources, the education. How could my father touch the world, coming from such a limited environment? There wasn't any sign of it, not a cloud in the sky, no people supporting him, had never been to seminary, didn't come from an influential family.

SPIRITUAL

"Your words have creative power. You give life to your faith by speaking it out."
–Joel

11 / GOD WILL MAKE THINGS HAPPEN THAT YOU COULDN'T MAKE HAPPEN.

But when you believe what you heard and not let people talk you out of it and take steps of faith, God will make things happen that you couldn't make happen. He'll open doors that no person can shut!

The question is, will you have the boldness to believe what you heard, even though all the circumstances say it's not possible? You heard you were going to have a baby, but the medical report says no way. You heard you were going to get your master's degree, but no one in your family has attended college. You heard your business was going to take off, but right now, you're struggling to pay your bills.

God puts things in your spirit as a seed. *If you discount it, say no way, that could never happen, then that seed will never take root.*

But when you do like Elijah, do like the lady with twins, do like my father and say, "God, I don't see a way, but I know You wouldn't have put this in me if You didn't have a way, Father, thank You that rain is coming.

- Thank You that healing is coming.
- Thank You that You're opening doors that I couldn't open.
- Thank You for bringing the right people across my path.
- Thank You for causing things to fall into place.
- Thank You for taking me where I couldn't go on my own.

DO THIS
In your quiet time, ask God if you've been limiting your prayers to what you can see. Ask Him to build your faith so the seeds can take root.

"Whatever you ask in prayer, believe that you have received it, and it will be yours." Mark 11:24, ESV

12 / YOU DON'T HAVE TO FIGURE OUT HOW IT'S GOING TO HAPPEN, ALL YOU HAVE TO DO IS BELIEVE.

Elijah's assistant said, "There's a little cloud starting to form." That little cloud turned into a huge cloud, and before long, there was an abundance of rain. Right there, Elijah saw what he'd heard in his spirit. That three-and-a-half-year drought came to an end.

You may not see how your dream could come to pass, how you could get well, how you could break the addiction. You know what you've heard, but you don't see any sign of it. Remember: **All it takes is a little cloud. A little favor. Just one right person, one healing, one good break, and suddenly you'll see what you heard.**

My father saw God open door after door. He founded Lakewood and was in the ministry over fifty years touching the world. When he would go back home, his parents were amazed. They couldn't believe all the favor and influence he had. They couldn't see it when he first mentioned it. They didn't think it was in him. When people aren't for you, don't get discouraged. They may not celebrate you until after the abundance of rain. That's okay. The main thing is this: **Don't let other people's doubt talk you out of what you've heard.**

"Don't let other people's doubt talk you out of what you've heard."
–Joel

13 / SOME OF THE THINGS GOD PUTS IN YOUR SPIRIT ARE NOT GOING TO MAKE SENSE TO PEOPLE. YOU HAVE TO BE WILLING TO BE MISUNDERSTOOD, TO BE CRITICIZED, TO BE TALKED ABOUT.

God told Noah to build a huge boat because there was going to be a great flood. What you may not realize is that it had never rained up to that point. The earth was watered from the dew on the ground. They had never seen water come down from the sky. It's common today. We've all seen floods. But Noah was building a boat, not next to the ocean, not on the shore, so he could easily get it in the water. No, he was building it on dry ground. And it wasn't a little fishing boat. God told him to build it four hundred and fifty feet long, a football field and a half. You can just imagine people coming by, shaking their heads, saying, "Noah, have you lost your mind, building a boat out in the middle of nowhere? You must be smoking some of these herbs." He was misunderstood, made fun of, talked about. It's no different today:

- "You're telling me you're going to have a baby? But it's been twenty years and the medical report says no way."
- "You're telling me you're going to touch the world? But you're a teenager on a farm, with no money, no education, no support."
- "You're telling me your child is going to do great things? But he spends half the year in detention."
- "You're telling me the city is going to sell you the Compaq Center and you're going to use it for a church?"

People may not understand. They may think you're far out, that you're not accepting reality. In one sense, it is not their fault. They didn't hear what you heard. Don't expect them to cheer you on. Don't expect them to agree with you. If you had to have them to fulfill your purpose, then they would agree with you. If they don't, then you don't need their support. You don't need their approval. You don't have to have their encouragement. Don't let them talk you out of what you heard.

> *Trust in the LORD with all your heart, and do not lean on your own understanding. In all your ways acknowledge him, and he will make straight your paths.* Proverbs 3:5–6, ESV

The enemy will use people, and sometimes good people, people you love and trust to plant doubt and negativity.

"**Are you sure** you're going to get well? The report doesn't look good."

"**Are you sure** you're going to get that position. There are three more-qualified people in front of you. Maybe in five years. I just don't see it now."

"**Are you sure** it's going to rain, Noah? By the way, what's rain? You're telling me that water is going to drop out of the sky and flood the earth? Noah, come back to reality. That's never happened before!"

14 / GOD IS GOING TO PUT THINGS IN YOUR SPIRIT THAT HAVE NEVER HAPPENED.

There will be things that your family has never seen — promotion, influence, new levels. You are coming into a day where you're going to see unprecedented favor, things bigger than you imagined, things that didn't seem possible. Remember, while you're believing for what God spoke to your spirit, you may be misunderstood. I'm sure Noah was the talk of the town: "Let's go see that crazy man out building a boat in the middle of the desert. He says it's going to rain." Noah didn't get offended. He knew they didn't hear what he heard. Don't be upset with the naysayers, people that don't support you. Just keep building, keep being your best, keep announcing it, keep thanking God. If you do this, I believe and declare, that what you hear in your spirit is going to override what you see with your eyes. Like Noah, God is going to do in your life what He's never done. You're coming into an abundance of rain, an abundance of health, an abundance of favor, an abundance of influence, in Jesus' name. /

YOUR SPIRITUAL STRENGTH, GOD'S MASTERPIECE

As it is written, "I have made you the father of many nations" — in the presence of the God in whom he believed, who gives life to the dead and calls into existence the things that do not exist.
ROMANS 4:17, ESV

For we live by faith, not by sight.
2 CORINTHIANS 5:7, NIV

When the angel of the LORD appeared to Gideon, he said, "The Lord is with you, mighty warrior."
JUDGES 6:12, NIV

Now may the God of peace who brought again from the dead our Lord Jesus, the great shepherd of the sheep, by the blood of the eternal covenant, equip you with everything good that you may do his will, working in us that which is pleasing in his sight, through Jesus Christ, to whom be glory forever and ever. Amen.
HEBREWS 13:20–21, ESV

What can be seen lasts only for a time, but what cannot be seen lasts forever.
2 CORINTHIANS 4:18, GNT

But the path of the just (righteous) is like light of dawn, that shines brighter and brighter until [it reaches its full strength and glory in] the perfect day.
PROVERBS 4:18, AMP

"See, I am doing a new thing! Now it springs up; do you not perceive it? I am making a way in the wilderness and streams in the wasteland."
ISAIAH 43:19, NIV

" . . . But as for me and my house, we will serve the LORD."
JOSHUA 24:15, NKJV

For we walk by faith, not by sight.
2 CORINTHIANS 5:7, ESV

Now faith is the substance of things hoped for, the evidence of things not seen.
HEBREWS 11:1, NKJV

The LORD will fulfill his purpose for me; your steadfast love, O LORD, endures forever. Do not forsake the work of your hands.
PSALM 138:8, ESV

"Whatever you ask in prayer, believe that you have received it, and it will be yours."
MARK 11:24, ESV

Trust in the Lord with all your heart, and do not lean on your own understanding. In all your ways acknowledge him, and he will make straight your paths.
PROVERBS 3:5–6, ESV

PROMISES / SPIRITUAL

1 / Think of a time, event, or situation where God spoke something to your spirit that seemed impossible. How did your faith help you in this experience?

2 / Has God ever spoken the opposite of your reality into your spirit, i.e., in a difficult situation? Take some time to quiet your mind, so you can hear what the Lord is saying to you right now.

3 / Think about something in your life that you want to be different. Maybe it's a job, a relationship, a bank balance. Now reflect on the reality that God "is doing a new thing" this very moment. In what ways can you prepare your spirit to receive His goodness?

4 / Have you been praying and believing a long time? What area of the prior section resonates most with you? Allow yourself to believe with fresh faith. Be an Elijah even if you're surrounded by people who don't agree.

5 / What do you want to thank God for today? As you give Him thanks, reflect on it in your spirit and your mind. What are you feeling as you do this? How does it strengthen your faith, believing with all your heart and soul that what God spoke to you will come to pass?

6 / Has God put a big dream, a big idea in your heart? What negative thoughts and doubts would stop you from moving forward if you let them? Picture yourself laying them down, letting God handle them in His own way.

WHAT IS GOD SAYING TO YOU?

NOTES / SPIRITUAL

NOTES / SPIRITUAL

NOTES / SPIRITUAL

NOTES / SPIRITUAL

Giving the world HOPE through our media outreaches!

Spotify **SiriusXM** SATELLITE RADIO

ROKU

For a full listing, visit
JoelOsteen.com/How-To-Watch

Stay connected, be blessed.

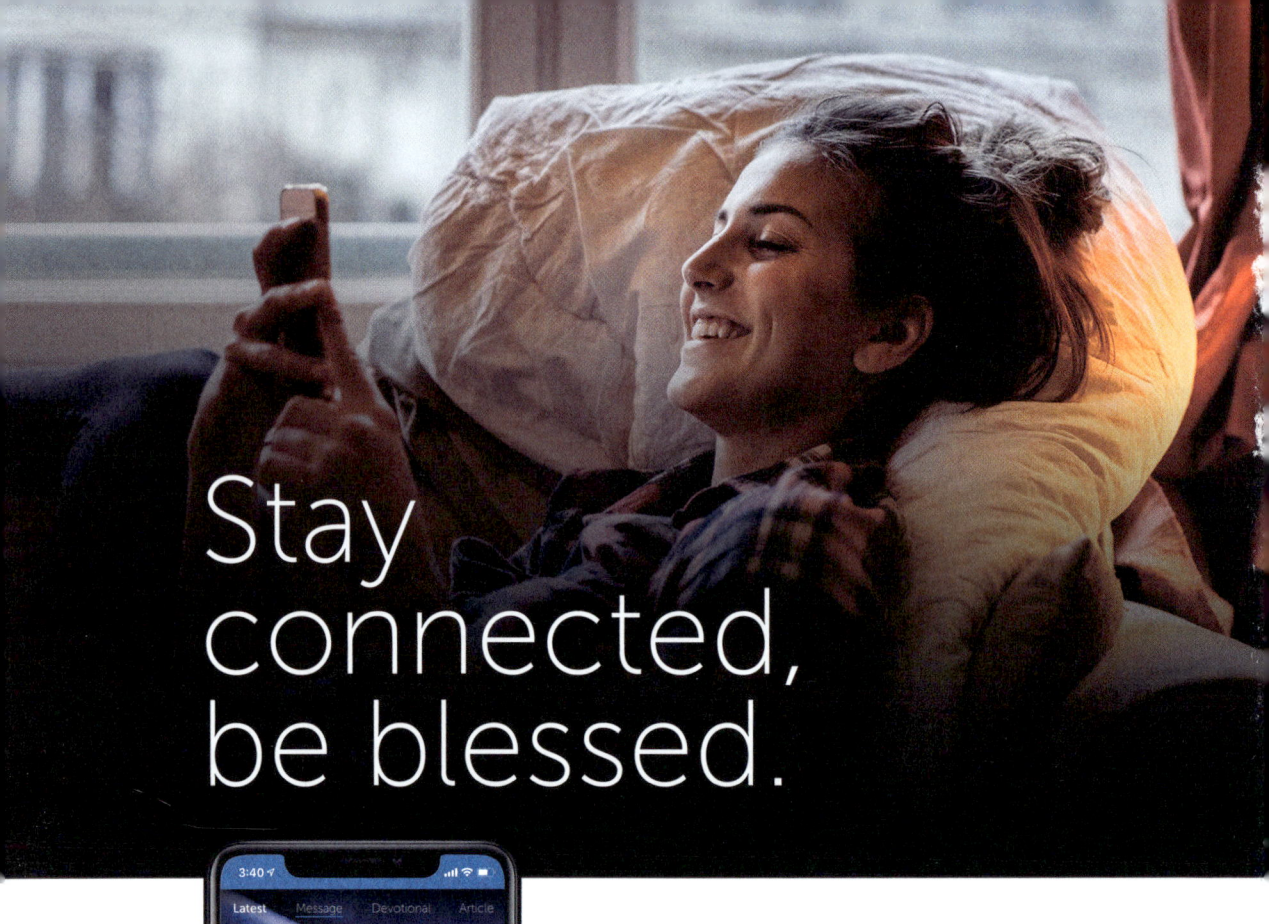

Get more from Joel & Victoria Osteen

It's time to step into the life of victory and favor that God has planned for you! Featuring new messages from Joel & Victoria Osteen, their free daily devotional and inspiring articles, hope is always at your fingertips with the free Joel Osteen app and online at JoelOsteen.com.

Get the app and visit us today at JoelOsteen.com.

Download on the App Store | GET IT ON Google Play

JOEL OSTEEN MINISTRIES

CONNECT WITH US